Equal Opportunities

Critical World Issues

CRITICAL WORLD ISSUES

Equal Opportunities

Frank McDowell

MASON CREST
PHILADELPHIA

Mason Crest
450 Parkway Drive, Suite D
Broomall, PA 19008
www.masoncrest.com

©2017 by Mason Crest, an imprint of National Highlights, Inc.

Printed and bound in the United States of America.

CPSIA Compliance Information: Batch #CWI2016.
For further information, contact Mason Crest at 1-866-MCP-Book.

First printing
1 3 5 7 9 8 6 4 2

Library of Congress Cataloging-in-Publication Data

on file at the Library of Congress
ISBN: 978-1-4222-3652-9 (hc)
ISBN: 978-1-4222-8132-1 (ebook)

Critical World Issues series ISBN: 978-1-4222-3645-1

Table of Contents

KEY ICONS TO LOOK FOR:

Words to Understand: These words with their easy-to-understand definitions will increase the reader's understanding of the text, while building vocabulary skills.

Sidebars: This boxed material within the main text allows readers to build knowledge, gain insights, explore possibilities, and broaden their perspectives by weaving together additional information to provide realistic and holistic perspectives.

Research Projects: Readers are pointed toward areas of further inquiry connected to each chapter. Suggestions are provided for projects that encourage deeper research and analysis.

Text-Dependent Questions: These questions send the reader back to the text for more careful attention to the evidence presented there.

Series Glossary of Key Terms: This back-of-the book glossary contains terminology used throughout this series. Words found here increase the reader's ability to read and comprehend higher-level books and articles in this field.

1

What Are Equal Opportunities?

Neil Walkingshaw is a car mechanic. He is 46 years old and lives in Scotland with his wife and young son, Sean. In November 2001, he won a landmark case at an *employment tribunal*—a special court in the United Kingdom (UK) that investigates serious disputes between employers and their employees.

Neil had worked full-time for the same employer for over eight years before his son was born. His wife, Tracy, also had a job. Like other women working in the UK, she was entitled to maternity leave—in her case, for six months. And, like many women, Tracy wanted to go back to work after her maternity leave was over.

Neil and Tracy planned to share the responsibility for looking after baby Sean, so Neil asked his employers if he could

Many people find it difficult to combine family life with a career.

work part-time. He said, "I expected the company to at least discuss the matter and look at all the options because women who had children had been offered their jobs part-time or other part-time jobs with the company, but I was told they couldn't get anyone to do it part-time along with me. I offered to try and find someone for a job share, and I was told the paperwork would be too complicated and too messy."

Neil felt he was left with no choice but to resign. Neil contacted the Equal Opportunities Commission, a body set up by the UK government in 1975 to enforce laws banning sex discrimination. They helped him take his case to the employment tribunal. The tribunal decided that Neil had been discriminated against and awarded him $54,511 in compensation. When giving their decision, members of the tribunal remarked that Neil's employers "gave no meaningful consideration" to his

 Words to Understand in This Chapter

civil rights—the rights that every person should have regardless of his or her sex, race, religion, ability status, or sexual orientation.

employment tribunal—a type of court in countries like the UK that has authority over workplace disputes.

ideology—the set of ideas and beliefs of a group or political party.

marital status—a person's state of being single, married, separated, divorced, or widowed.

person of color—a person who is not white or of European parentage.

sexual orientation—a person's sexual identity in relation to the gender to which they are attracted: heterosexual, homosexual, or bisexual.

Women have proven themselves capable of doing many different kinds of work, in spite of traditional, stereotyped opinions.

request to work part-time. They added that if a woman had made the same request, the company would probably have agreed.

After hearing the tribunal's decision, Neil commented: "I'm glad I did this because there will be other guys in the same position who want to look after their kids. I hope this will encourage them to make sure they can do that." Today, Neil works part-time for a different car repair company—and enjoys his other part-time task of looking after Sean.

Reasons for Discrimination

Gender is not the only area in the world in which people suffer from a lack of equal opportunities:

Race and Ethnicity: People face challenges in getting equal job opportunities and equal pay, regardless of their skills and experience, because of the color of their skin or their cultural background.

Disability: Many people with disabilities who have attained high academic qualifications find that success in their studies does not necessarily lead to a rewarding career—or, in some cases, to any job at all.

Age: Older people are often assumed to be less productive than younger workers. In times of economic crisis, they are usually among the first to be laid off. In industrial societies, it can be particularly difficult for people over the age of 50 to find a job.

Religious Beliefs: In different parts of the world, there is mistreatment and even violence against people who believe in a religion that is different from the majority. In addition to facing hostility, they may be discriminated against at work and find it difficult to practice their faith if the workplace is unaccommodating.

Sexual Orientation: People who are lesbian, gay, bisexual, or transgender may experience harassment, isolation, and discrimination from employers and coworkers because of their sexual orientation.

Defining "Equal Opportunity"

The idea of "equal opportunities" is closely linked to other important values about how life should be lived—such as justice and tolerance. It involves sensitive issues, including gender, race, religion, disability, sexual orientation, and age. It affects all levels of society, from government lawmakers to children at school.

Equal opportunities can mean different things, based on who is involved and where they are. But whoever—and wherever—they are, most people agree that equal opportunities means giving people *civil rights*, or equal rights in employment and education as well as a fair chance to make the best of their lives regardless of characteristics like gender, race, age, disability, or religion.

Accepting peoples' *sexual orientation* (whether they are gay, straight, or bisexual), *marital status* (single, married, divorced, or widowed), and family status (having children or not) is also included in definitions of equal opportunities.

Do We Have Equal Opportunities?

Most people think equal opportunities are important, but equality is seldom achieved—at least, not completely. Law makers and campaigners do not all agree on how equal rights should be introduced or enforced. Also, many individuals still benefit from unequal opportunities in business or in institutions such as the courts and armed forces, where being of a certain race, gender, or sexual orientation may provide greater influence and chances to advance. Often, those are the people with the most power to create change, but until they are willing to question some of their work practices and perhaps give up some of their privileges, it will be difficult to create a level playing field for all.

Anti-discrimination activists continue to campaign, and as a result, many countries have passed equal opportunities laws. In this book, we will investigate how equal opportunities policies are changing the way in which men and women work in many parts of the world.

Equality Through the Law

Today, many countries have laws giving equal rights to male and female workers and to particular groups of employees, such as people with disabilities. They also have laws banning racial discrimination in all areas of life, including work and education. Some countries have laws protecting religious minorities from harassment in the workplace and elsewhere.

Before the 1960s in the United States, there were few equal opportunities laws because most policy makers thought they were unnecessary. Some thought equal rights was a moral issue that individuals should decide for themselves. Others believed that laws would not work since they could not change peoples' attitudes. Still others refused to give up old prejudices, saying that equity policies would destroy "traditional ways of life."

Some politicians hoped that discrimination would gradually vanish from the workplace—and the whole of society—as men and women began to work for the same companies, and people from different ethnic groups moved to the same neighborhoods. They believed that as different people came to know each other, they would become accepting of each culture and

Until the 1960s, many places in the United States were segregated, with separate theaters, schools, hospitals, and other public facilities for whites and African-Americans.

gender and eventually behave in a fair, equal way. Others thought that the free market would create equal opportunities: businesses would not care whether employees were male or female, gay or straight, black or white, old or young, with disabilities or without, as long as they worked productively.

Despite hopes that equity would increase in society, discrimination continued. Almost everywhere, top jobs were given to able-bodied white men. Women and *people of color* were still working mainly in low-status, poorly paid jobs. People with disabilities and those over 50 found it hard to get work at all.

Campaigners came to realize that civil rights would never be achieved by merely hoping that systems of employment and education would correct themselves. Discrimination was not a private moral issue for individuals alone. It was a political problem that affected everyone. Equality at work could only be achieved by changing the balance of power within society— and that would require new laws.

The Equal Opportunity Movement

During the 1950s and 1960s, several factors combined to make governments in the United States and Europe think more carefully about how different groups in society should be protected by law.

By the 1960s, Western industrial economies were growing quickly. Companies needed good employees and were prepared to treat them well. There was also a new generation of well-educated young people who wanted rewarding careers. Young men were not prepared to settle for low-paying, menial jobs, and young women did not all want to be mothers and home-makers.

The terrible experiences of World War II had led to support for peaceful international organizations, such as the United Nations (UN), and an interest in human rights of all kinds— including equal opportunities. In some European countries, such as Sweden and Denmark, progressive political attitudes and the development of the welfare state enabled women to work on almost equal terms with men—although less was done to help ethnic minorities.

In the United States, people of color—including African-Americans, Native Americans, Asians, and Latinos—faced unequal treatment at work and in their everyday lives. From 1955 forward, African-Americans staged nonviolent protests against discrimination, launching the civil rights movement. In 1963, led by the inspirational preacher and social activist Martin Luther King, they joined with many thousands of white supporters and other people of color in mass demonstrations demanding equal treatment. They persuaded the government to pass the most important equal opportunities law

Activists like Martin Luther King Jr. struggled for many years to get rights for African Americans that were equal to those of their white fellow-citizens.

in US history, the Civil Rights Act of 1964, which outlawed discrimination based on race, color, religion, sex, or national origin. From then on, it was illegal to have segregation or unequal treatment in schools, workplaces, voting, and places that served the general public like restaurants and stores.

American women played a key part in civil rights protests and also made demands of their own. Since 1923, female politicians had been leading campaigns calling for the Equal Rights

Amendment (ERA) to the US Constitution, which would give women legal equality with men. By the 1960s, they had been joined by radical feminists, who called for a complete change in traditional gender roles, family life, and employer practices. In 1963, women won the right to equal pay for equal work with the passage of the Equal Pay Act. Further employment rights were guaranteed by the Civil Rights Act the following year.

In the years following the Civil Rights Act, laws were introduced in the US banning job discrimination against people

President Lyndon B. Johnson signs the Civil Rights Act of 1964 in the White House. This landmark legislation prohibited discrimination on the basis of race, color, religion, sex, or national origin.

With banners demanding equality, women march through in Washington, D.C., 1970.

who had disabilities and those over 40 years old. Partiality based on religion was also deemed illegal. Since 1991, Americans who feel they have suffered discrimination have been able to seek financial damages. Other countries, including Canada, Australia, and many in the European Union (EU), have followed this example.

What Is the Role of Culture and Religion?

Cultural norms in different countries, often shaped by religious *ideologies*, can be additional factors that affect equal opportunities. A nation's people may believe their own laws will produce the best life for all their workers. The Taliban rulers of Afghanistan received worldwide criticism for their treatment of women—such as banning female nurses and teachers from work—until their removal from power in 2002.

According to a 2013 study by the World Bank, the world's lowest percentages of women aged 15 years or older working for wages are in Algeria and Iraq (15 percent of the workforce in each), followed by Afghanistan and Jordan (each 16 percent). In all of these countries, strict interpretations of Islam are held by those in power.

A 2014 *Washington Post* article supported the finding that women work least frequently in the Middle East and broader Muslim world. While this is not true in all Muslim-majority countries, it is still a notable distinction. Part of this is reflected in rising unemployment overall in some of these countries, but with fewer than one in four women at work in many of them, there are also cultural and religious components at work.

Has Political Change Created Equality?

During the twentieth century, there were revolutions in many parts of the world. New left-wing and communist governments claimed to be fighting for equality for all their citizens. Many people hoped that such political movements would bring equal opportunities more quickly than new laws. However, looking back, many changes made in the name of "equality" failed to bring fundamental freedoms to the public.

For example, after the Russian Revolution in 1917, women in the Soviet Union were given equal political rights with men. They had the right to work outside the home and receive a good education. State-run industries relied on women working

Russian men and women work on a railroad line in Petrograd, 1922. The Bolsheviks promoted the ideal of women's equality in the Soviet Union, but this novel idea was not well implemented.

side-by-side with men, and female workers were praised as "real Soviet women, proud to be good mothers and good workers." But at the same time, Soviet laws restricted individual freedoms such as the right to protest against the government and the right to set up one's own business.

After World War II, many Soviet women trained for skilled professional careers. While their job options expanded, they were still never paid as much as men. Also, like Soviet women working on farms and in factories, they were expected to run a home and care for children as well as work full-time.

Women make clothes in a textile shop in eastern China. Although communist theory teaches that women are equal with men, traditional Chinese attitudes toward women have proven to be stronger than political ideology.

The 1948 Communist Revolution in China also promised equality for its citizens, but political change failed to alter traditional attitudes toward women. As one observer commented: "Chinese parents want boys rather than girls, so from the moment they are born, females are made to feel unwanted. In later life, they may be married off to an older, abusive husband, or even sold."

In the late twentieth century, both China and Russia (after the break-up of the Soviet Union) introduced capitalist economic policies. These encouraged "freedom" and "enterprise," but they also had a damaging effect on women and other disadvantaged groups. For example, in 1995, women's wages in Russia were 40 percent of men's, compared to 70 percent during the Soviet-Union era.

Since 1995, large numbers of Chinese men have left the countryside to find better-paying jobs in cities, leaving women to do over 70 percent of the work on farms. The government's new economic rules mean that farm prices have fallen dramatically, and many female farmers simply cannot earn enough to survive. The Beijing Suicide Research and Prevention Center reported in 2009 that the suicide rate for females in China was three times higher than that for males.

 Text-Dependent Questions

1. Name eight different characteristics about a person that are included in the definition of equal opportunities.
2. Describe the events from 1955 to 1964 that led to the Civil Rights Act being passed.

 Research Project

Using the Internet or your school library, research the topic of civil rights laws, and answer the following question: "Should there be civil rights laws to give people equal opportunities?"

Some claim that it is essential that everyone is given the same opportunities in school, work, and life in general. Civil rights laws are the only way to ensure this will happen because they can be enforced by the authorities.

Others contend that societies naturally do what works best for them. No civil rights laws are necessary because people should be able to make their own decisions about how to treat other people. If they don't want to treat others fairly, that is up to them and not the government.

Write a two-page report, using data you have found in your research to support your conclusion, and present it to your class.

Working Women and Working Men

Despite the introduction of equal opportunities laws, it is still difficult to find a country where the majority of female workers are treated completely equally with men. Although there are many successful working women—and some outstanding high achievers—female workers almost always receive lower pay overall than male workers.

In the United States, for example, the American Association of University Women (AAUW) reported that in 2014, women working full time earned only 79 percent of what men earned. The gap has narrowed since the 1970s, due largely to women's progress in education and joining the workforce as well as men's wages rising at a slower rate. However, progress has slowed down in recent years, and the pay gap will likely remain unless interventions are made.

Despite equal opportunities laws, the average woman's pay in the United States is still much lower than men's.

A woman secretary and her male boss, 1950s. Working women faced discrimination because many employers assumed that they were "naturally" more suited to clerical work that supported male executives.

Around the world, the types of jobs that women work in are generally less skilled and therefore less secure than the work performed by men. Women are less likely than men to belong to *labor unions*, organized workers' groups that can bargain for pay raises and protect their rights. They are much more likely than men to be employed on temporary or part-time contracts.

 Words to Understand in This Chapter

labor union—an organization of workers formed to protect the rights and interests of its members.

piecework—work in which one is paid for each thing they make or do, not for the amount of time they work.

In economic crises, women and older people are the groups most likely to be unemployed. In some countries, women are treated as pools of "disposable" labor—if their job contract ends, their husbands or their parents are expected to support them. In many nations, only men are expected to earn a steady "family wage."

Women Workers

Since the 1970s, increasing numbers of women have worked for wages. In the late 1990s, women made up about 36 percent of the wage-earning workforce worldwide, but in 2010, the UN

These women in New York City are members of a labor union, an organization that is supposed to protect the rights of workers. Women and men are often treated differently in the workplace.

Department of Economic and Social Affairs reported a rise to 52 percent, compared to 77 percent for men. Still, many women work at home, often unpaid, and are not wage earners in the job market. Some follow traditional occupations, such as

In the Zone

An Export Processing Zone (EPZ) is a tax-free industrial area where foreign companies set up factories. Governments eager to attract companies to these zones often ban labor unions. They may also suspend laws protecting workers' rights, including those regarding health and safety. Wages are often low, hours are long, and there is poor job security. In her 2010 report, *Women Working in the Shadows*, Ingeborg Wick documented 130 countries with EPZs out of 196 in the world. An estimated 70 percent of the workers are women, with companies specifically targeting women up to 25 years old who are unmarried and have no children.

Women peel and process fresh raw shrimps for export in a seafood factory in a Vietnam. Conditions for workers in Export Processing Zones are often poor.

farming or craftwork. Others help their parents or husbands by working in small family enterprises.

As economic globalization increases, and multinational corporations search for the cheapest, least powerful employees, large numbers of women are being employed in low-paid *piecework* in their homes or in cramped, unhealthy conditions, and they are oftentimes not entitled to any benefits.

What Is Women's Work?

In every country, certain jobs are stereotypically referred to as "women's work," while others are believed to "belong" to men. But these ideas generally vary from country to country. Whether a job is considered "male" or "female" depends on local customs and traditions. These can sometimes be surprising to those with different gender norms. In India, for example, women work as road-builders—a typical "man's job" in many other parts of the world.

The jobs most frequently done by women around the world have developed from women's traditional tasks within the household, such as nursing, teaching, and childcare. Caring for the sick and educating children are obviously responsible and important jobs, yet they often

In 2001, police officer Michelle Chew, a mother, won a case against her employers after they insisted that she work early-morning, late-evening, and nighttime shifts. The court decided that this amounted to sex discrimination against women, who typically have greater childcare responsibilities than men.

have low status and poor prospects because they are done by women. The same is true for most other occupations seen as "women's work." In positions where women work in jobs that are also done by men, they generally occupy the least senior positions.

Pay Inequality

Because of their low status, jobs labeled as "women's work" are usually poorly paid. Even where men and women do similar jobs, they often do not receive equal pay. Women in countries with equal opportunities laws have successfully challenged this several times. In one famous case, a group of school lunchroom monitors in the UK won the right to be treated as permanent employees like the garbage collectors employed by the same organization. This entitled them to benefits such as vacation pay.

Still, discrimination against women in pay remains. The AAUW reported that within each race in 2014, white women earned an average of 78 percent of what white men earned, Asian women earned 79 percent compared to Asian men, Latina women earned 89 percent, and African American women earned 90 percent. Even measuring at the highest levels of educational degrees, the pay gap still persists at similar rates.

Latina and African-American women find themselves doubly disadvantaged due to gender and race. If women of different races are compared only to white men, the statistics reveal that gender and race lead to a further discrepancy in pay: Latina women earned 54 percent of what white men earned, and African-American women earned 63 percent.

Fewer Opportunities

In most countries, women have a more narrow choice of jobs than men. Women have traditionally worked in a limited number of occupations, and this pattern continues even in countries where there are equal opportunities laws.

President Barack Obama signs an executive order to strengthen enforcement of equal pay laws for women, at an event marking Equal Pay Day in the White House, April 8, 2014. Among those standing with the president is Lilly Ledbetter, who filed an influential employment discrimination lawsuit against her employer, Goodyear Tire, after finding out that during her twenty years as a manager she had been paid less than male employees for doing the same work. Although her lawsuit was initially successful, the Supreme Court later ruled that Ledbetter could not collect damages because the Title VII of the Civil Rights Act of 1964, which made it illegal for businesses to discriminate against women or minorities in employment, had required claims to be filed within a 180-day period. In response, the US Congress passed the Lilly Ledbetter Fair Pay Act of 2009 to close this loophole in the Civil Rights Act. The Lilly Ledbetter Fair Pay Act was the first bill that President Obama signed into law after taking office in January 2009.

In the past, it was often assumed by women's families and employers that certain occupations were not suitable for them. Reasons for this included the idea that women were physically or mentally weaker, sometimes backed up by religious arguments or medical taboos.

In a few countries—including Bolivia, Lesotho, Syria, and Zaire—husbands still have the right to ban their wives' choice

The "Maid Trade"

Some female employees are treated with a great deal of disrespect by their employers and are at risk of sexual harassment and physical abuse. The "maid trade" provides a good example: more than 1.5 million Asian women work as household servants—typically cooking and cleaning—in the Middle East and in rich Asian regions such as Hong Kong. Most do not speak the local language and are ignorant of the law. They may be isolated within their employers' homes with little control over their lives, and many have alleged that their employers treat them poorly.

A large number of women have been tricked into applying for jobs as maids, then forced to work as prostitutes, where men usually maintain power and control with violence. Other women end up in prostitution because their poor families may hand them to dealers who promise to find them work without saying what it will be.

of work or to forbid them from going out to work at all. Besides unfair attitudes, three other factors that make work choice a challenge for women are lack of education, limited access to funding, and women's domestic responsibilities.

The US Bureau of Labor Statistics stated that from 1972 to 2012, the percentage of female American workers in the traditionally "female work" of education and health services is comprised of 76.7 percent women. The percentage of women in government work rose from 42.7 to 56.8 and in retail/wholesale trade from 38.1 to 43.6 percent. While this represents growing opportunities for women, they still have difficulty breaking into sectors like manufacturing (27.3 percent female) and transport/warehousing (23.1 percent).

Why Is Education Important?

Literacy data from the United Nations Educational, Scientific, and Cultural Organization (UNESCO) showed that in 2013, 774 million adults 15 years and older still could not read or write. Two-thirds of these adults (493 million people) are women. Among youth, 123 million are illiterate, 76 million of whom are female. Even though the size of the global illiterate population is shrinking, the female share of the illiterate population has remained virtually steady at 63 to 64 percent.

In most poor countries, fewer girls than boys go to school, and they stay in education for a shorter length of time. This is either because they are believed to be "not worth" educating—when they marry, they would leave the family home—or because they are needed to help around the home or care for younger siblings. The 2012 World Development Report on

Gender Equality and Development showed boys remain 1.55 times more likely to complete secondary education than girls in Africa and South Asia.

Is Poverty a Factor?

In some countries, poverty, inheritance laws, and traditional customs restrict women's access to land or other forms of wealth. This limits their chances of going into business for themselves. Even in countries with equal opportunities laws, women complain that it is much harder for them to borrow money to start a company than it would be for a man.

Where poverty is combined with domestic responsibilities, a career can be impossible. Many women in poor rural communities spend their time caring for children, growing food, and performing chores such as gathering firewood or collecting water. They may work all day long, but not for pay. In contrast, working women enjoy a much higher quality of life in industrialized regions such as the EU, but even they often find their opportunities limited by the need to care for homes and families.

Successful Career Women and the "Glass Ceiling"

There are increasing numbers of successful career women in Western nations, but they remain a minority compared with successful men. In the United States, for example, only 33 percent of judges are women.

Lack of education means that most women worldwide have little chance of competing with men. But even in countries such as the United States, Portugal, and the United Kingdom—where there are now more female university students than male—many intelligent, ambitious women still are not as successful as men in their careers. Most women find it very difficult to combine a career with having children and leading a "normal" family life. Long hours, night shifts, and the difficulty of finding reliable childcare create serious problems for working mothers—especially if they are single parents.

Successful career women also complain of peoples' attitudes against them. Many say that they feel excluded from the traditional male work culture—not just in physically demand-

According to the US Education Department, more than 76 percent of all public school teachers are women. The percentage of female teachers is even higher at the elementary school level, roughly 84 percent.

ing jobs such as construction, but also among groups of senior male executives. Women use terms like "sticky floor" and "glass ceiling" to describe the invisible barriers of suspicion and prejudice by male managers that they feel stand in the way of their progress.

Successful women also face criticism, and sometimes open hostility, from colleagues. Some women find that men feel threatened by the female "invasion" of their male work environment and resent having to take orders from women with power. Some men allege that women are not tough enough to compete in the male world of big business—or alternatively complain that successful women are unnaturally hard and "unfeminine."

But equal opportunities are very complex—not only men, but also women without children, employed by companies with equal opportunities policies have recently complained that working mothers receive unfair advantages.

Changing Times

At the start of the new millennium, there is no denying that women's working lives are very different from 50 years before. In industrialized countries, women have proven that they can succeed in a wide range of traditionally male roles, from astronauts and airline pilots to surgeons and sports superstars. Women with business skills now set up their own companies and find work in new kinds of careers such as communications and media.

However, women are still a small minority in higher-level positions compared to men. In the United States in 2014, for

According to the U.S. Department of Labor, in 2015 women made up about 47 percent of the labor force. However, despite laws outlawing discrimination on the basis of gender, it has been difficult for women to break through the "glass ceiling" and achieve promotion to the most powerful, prestigious, and highest-paying positions.

example, women held almost 52 percent of all professional-level jobs but only 14.6 percent were executive officers, 8.1 percent top earners, and 4.6 percent CEOs of Fortune 500 companies, according to the Center for American Progress.

In developing countries, educated women can train as doctors and college lecturers. By the mid-1990s, around half of all university teachers in Cuba, Namibia, Thailand, and several islands in the Caribbean were women.

Women in South America, Africa, and Asia have also broadened business prospects by joining together in cooperative schemes to harvest and market farm produce and craftwork. In order to help finance these businesses, they have set up a special network of banks that offer small loans to women. Over 90 percent of the Grameen Bank of Bangladesh's clients are women. The Self-Employed Women's Association Co-operative Bank of India lends to women only. Worldwide, women's banks help over half a million customers each year.

Even with these advances for women, the World Economic Forum estimates that, at the current rate of

Meg Whitman, the chief executive officer (CEO) of the technology company Hewlett Packard, is an example of a female executive who has risen to the highest level. She previously ran the online auction firm eBay; during her ten-year term revenue grew from $4 million to $8 billion. Whitman was inducted into the U.S. Business Hall of Fame in 2008.

progress, women worldwide will have to wait until the year 2095 to achieve equality with men in the workplace.

Women in Politics

Women have become more involved in politics of all kinds—from radical protest groups to mainstream political parties. But most women in politics serve as ordinary members of Congress or other assemblies, where they are usually in a minority. In 2015, for example, women held 19.4 percent of seats in the US Congress and 29 percent of the UK's Parliament. Worldwide, women represent 22 percent of the members elected to democratic parliaments.

However, a few tough and ambitious women have risen to become heads of government. These include Golda Meir, who served as prime minister of Israel from 1969 to 1974; Margaret Thatcher, prime minister of the United Kingdom from 1979 to 1990; and Benazir Bhutto, prime minister of Pakistan from

Angela Merkel has served as chancellor of Germany since 2005. Many people consider her one of the most important and influential female politicians in the world. Merkel is well educated, having earned a university doctorate and working as a research scientist before entering politics.

Hillary Clinton has been one of the most influential women in American politics, having served in the US Senate and as the Secretary of State and waging historic campaigns for the presidency in 2008 and 2016.

1988 to 1990 and again from 1993 to 1996. In January 2016, there were 22 female presidents, prime ministers, or heads of state in the world. Slowly, female politicians have helped to improve equal opportunities in many countries. As Texas politician Sissy Farenthold once declared, "You change laws by changing law makers."

 ## Text-Dependent Questions

1. Explain why Export Processing Zones often have poor, unsafe working conditions for women.
2. What are three reasons the "glass ceiling" limits successful women from advancing?

 ## Research Project

Using the Internet or your school library, research the topic of women's rights in the workplace, and answer the following question: "Should working mothers have more influence in scheduling their work times than others because of their childcare duties at home?"

Some believe women with children have little choice about their home schedules because of childcare obligations. They have to be home with their children, especially outside of their kids' school hours, or they need to pay for childcare, which can be expensive. They should have more say in their work schedules.

Others argue that everyone, with or without children, have obligations that they need to take care of, and women with children should not be given special privileges in scheduling work. That would allow for those women to possibly take advantage of the system or breed resentment among coworkers who may have legitimate home responsibilities themselves.

Write a two-page report, using data you have found in your research to support your conclusion, and present it to your class.

3

Racial Discrimination

According to biologists, there is only one *race* of people—the human race. Yet everywhere, men and women discriminate against others that they think are different from themselves—in nationality, culture, language, skin color, or membership in a clan or tribe. Race refers to a group of people with shared distinctive physical traits. *Ethnicity* is more complex, as it refers to a group with common racial, national, tribal, religious, linguistic, or cultural backgrounds. Two people may both be Asian by race, but with regard to ethnicity, one may be Korean and the other Indian.

Often, there is discrimination by majority communities against minorities who live in the same area. During the rule of Saddam Hussein in Iraq, there was discrimination against Kurdish minorities for many years. In the past, especially in

People in Oakland, California, march to draw attention to the killings of several African Americans by police as part of the Black Lives Matter campaign. African Americans have long protested that they are discriminated against by police in the United States.

41

Australia, the Americas, and many territories of the British Empire, colonists arrived in a new land, imposed their own laws and culture, and took over the native peoples' lands. This led to a history of discrimination against native peoples.

Racial discrimination results from ignorance regarding a group of people and their culture. It is also closely linked to power in almost all cases: people who have jobs, land, or wealth rarely want to give them up, and they sometimes fear that anyone who is "different" will take these things from them. In Germany, for example, until the year 2000, workers of Turkish origin did not have the right to full citizenship, even though they were born and educated in Germany, worked there, and paid taxes.

People in power sometimes persuade themselves that those from different backgrounds are incapable of high achievement because they are uneducated, less "civilized," or lacking in

 Words to Understand in This Chapter

affirmative action—the practice of improving the educational and job opportunities for members of groups that have not been treated fairly in the past because of their race, sex, etc.

apartheid—a former social system in South Africa in which black people and people from other racial groups did not have the same political and economic rights as white people and were forced to live separately from white people.

ethnicity—a group of people with common racial, national, tribal, religious, linguistic, or cultural backgrounds.

race—any one of the groups that human beings can be divided into based on shared distinctive physical traits.

experience. In 2001, the UK had only 12 members of Parliament (MPs) who were people of color, representing 1.8 percent of the total. If MPs had been elected to reflect the proportions of different groups among voters, there should have been 40. There has been progress by 2015, with 42 non-white MPs, or 6.6 percent of the total.

The fight for equal opportunities has been backed by politicians and community leaders who argue that each person should be respected as an individual human being. Many religious leaders have taught that a person's worth has to do with character qualities such as kindness or devotion to duty, and national origin and culture can add to the richness of a community. However, people from minority communities continue to face discrimination in housing, schooling, health care, and work despite civil rights laws prohibiting unequal treatment.

Racial Discrimination in History

From the sixteenth century on, European colonists settled in countries all over the world. Some Europeans sincerely believed they were bringing "civilization" to native people groups. Others used this idea to disguise their real motives—seeking wealth and political power. As a result, many local peoples suffered. Their economies were disrupted and their traditional skills devalued. They lost control of their lands and were denied education and health care.

When Europeans first settled in South America, religious scholars actually discussed whether the indigenous people were truly human and whether they had souls. These were not just religious concerns. By treating local people as inferior,

Members of the Ku Klux Klan at a cross burning in Tennessee, 1948. The Klan was an organization created to defend "white rights" and terrorize African Americans, particularly in the South.

European settlers were able to claim that they were "helping" them by taking over their lands. This view of non-Europeans as subhuman was also used to justify the thriving trade of black slaves from Africa to the US and the Caribbean. This was one of the most heinous examples of racial mistreatment in world history, and it has a lasting impact of the African American community even today.

Slavery was abolished in the United States in 1865 after the Civil War. Although racist attitudes and practices were increasingly condemned, they did not go away. Millions of African American citizens were left poor, uneducated, and in low-level jobs. By the middle of the twentieth century, European countries were losing their empires but maintained close ties with the countries they had once ruled. When there was a labor shortage in the UK after World War II, workers were recruited from the Indian subcontinent and the Caribbean. These workers, however, were not welcomed as equals when they arrived. Today, some of these workers, including the Roma, are still disadvantaged in housing, education, health care—and equal opportunities at work.

A great number of those who arrived in the UK from the Caribbean after 1945 found work on the buses and railroads. Today, many of their descendants are still working in public transportation, mostly in low-paying jobs. There are about 20 million white males in the UK and around half a million Afro-Caribbean males, yet 18 percent of Afro-Caribbean men work in transportation, compared to only 9 percent of white men.

Apartheid and Multiculturalism

From 1948 to 1994, the white South African government had a policy called *apartheid*, or racial separation. People were classified as black, white, colored, or Indian, and the majority non-white population was forced to live in separate communities and use separate public facilities. They were denied basic civil rights, and millions were forced from their homes and jobs, having to resettle in "homelands"—barren regions lacking roads, power, water sources, farms, and industries; very few schools, hospitals, and opportunities for paid work were available as well.

Protesters carry coffins representing people killed by the South African police at the township of Sharpeville in 1960, during the apartheid regime.

With internal uprisings and pressure from the international community, white president Frederik Willem de Klerk initiated policies to end apartheid in 1990. That year, black social activist and political leader Nelson Mandela was freed after 27 years in prison for rebelling against the government. He became the first black president of South Africa in 1994 and formed a multiethnic government that transitioned the country out of apartheid and toward equality. Mandela and de Klerk were jointly awarded the 1993 Nobel Peace Prize "for their work for the peaceful termination of the apartheid regime, and for laying the foundations for a new democratic South Africa."

Many societies now claim to be multicultural, and this is usually assumed to be a good thing. Being multicultural means respecting different peoples' beliefs and traditions, giving them equal importance, and making sure that none of them oppresses the others. The aim is to promote tolerance and understanding, and to increase each community member's sense of security and self-confidence. However, equal opportunities campaigners have recently questioned whether multiculturalism really does help end racism and discrimination.

Nelson Mandela (seated) signs the oath of office as he assumes the presidency of South Africa after the country's first all-race elections, May 1994.

Racism in Multicultural Societies

Some people argue that proponents of multiculturalism do not look deeply enough at the causes of racial discrimination. They contend that multicultural policies may allow for different ethnic groups living in the same region, but they end up divided into separate communities.

Families with the same ethnic background often live close together. At an individual level, this may bring benefits: people find it convenient to be near stores selling their preferred foods, clothes, literature, and music as well as have their own place of worship nearby. But for society as a whole, this can lead to problematic divisions and sometimes outbreaks of violence between rival groups who are intolerant of one another's way of life. These divisions between separate communities are often continued in the workplace, leading to a lack of career

 Black Is Beautiful

In the 1960s and 1970s, some African Americans felt dissatisfied with the progress made by the civil rights movement—even after new equal opportunities laws had been passed. They launched the Black Power movement for black people to campaign in a more militant fashion. They argued that African Americans should stop protesting alongside liberal whites and instead use all their energy to focus on their own communities. They campaigned to win greater respect for black culture, using slogans such as "Black is beautiful."

opportunities for some people and racial stereotyping.

Keeping people separate can also lead to abuses. For example, many Asian women work in Western countries as sewing-machinists and garment makers. They often perform this work in their own homes or in cramped factories known as sweat-shops (often owned by Asian businessmen). Many are exploited and underpaid because they are isolated and do not belong to trade unions or other organizations that might be able to protect them. Some do not speak the language and many have no knowledge of how to complain or assert their right to equal opportunities.

What Is Institutional Racism?

In most countries today, the most powerful racial group controls the important state institutions—from schools and government to the army and police. Even if these institutions do not deliberately discriminate against any group in society and do not intend to be racist, they may still foster unequal treatment.

Institutional racism has been described as "policies and procedures within institutions that deny equal treatment to members of ethnic minority groups." Valerie Amos, formerly Chief Executive of the Equal Opportunities Commission, explains: "Historically, an environment has existed in which the favoring of individuals from certain groups (e.g. white men) has not been challenged because it is a norm. So, 'negative' discrimination, in favor of particular groups, became institutionalized."

Civil rights activists have long claimed that institutional racism exists. Examples include school tests tailored to white

A Gallup Poll taken in August 2015 found that 25 percent of Hispanic Americans report-
ed experiencing discrimination because of their ethnicity at work, in dealings with police,
while getting healthcare, or at a bar or restaurant. Hispanic immigrants were more likely
to be discriminated against than were those who were born in the United States, the Gallup
Poll found.

culture and the higher percentage of white bosses leading to a
higher percentage of white employees. In the UK, campaigners
won support after investigations into one of the country's most
important institutions, the police. In the 1990s, the
Metropolitan Police Force was accused of institutional racism
for failing to act after a black student, Stephen Lawrence, was
murdered in London in a random, unprovoked attack by a

group of young, white, racist males. Government statistics show that Asians in the UK are 50 times more likely to suffer racist attacks than whites, and Afro-Caribbeans 36 times more likely.

More recently, in the United States there have been protests about the killing of unarmed African Americans by police. The death of teenager Michael Brown in 2014 at the hands of a police officer in Ferguson, Missouri, led to riots and drew national attention to the issue. Thanks to the Twitter app, the hashtag #BlackLivesMatter became instantly popular. Protests and marches to draw attention to the issue have continued as other African Americans have been killed by police actions or died while in police custody, including Tamir Rice, Eric Harris, and Freddie Gray.

Equal Job Opportunities

Many equal opportunities campaigners argue that simply offering people equal chances to apply for jobs still discriminates against disadvantaged groups in society. They say that marginalized people need to be given extra help to get a good education and learn useful skills. Otherwise, they will remain at a disadvantage in their search for work.

To ensure that everyone really does have an equal chance at a rewarding career, campaigners for equal opportunities suggest *affirmative action*, a policy that favors people of disadvantaged groups. This might include increasing access to higher education or addressing disparities in job opportunities and pay for people of color, women, or any other group that suffers discrimination. It might also involve cultural, legal, and financial reforms to remove prejudice and inequality from society as a whole. Campaigners argue that equal opportunities policies should be judged not by their good intentions but by their practical results.

In one workplace discrimination case, two Pakistani men living in the UK were asked to complete application forms in their own handwriting for manual labor jobs at a car manufacturing company. This was the company's standard procedure for all people applying to work for them. However, neither of the men could read and write in English, so they were unable to complete the forms and did not get the jobs. The authorities decided that the company was guilty of racial discrimination because being literate in English was not a necessary qualification for manual labor.

Success and Challenges

In Europe, the US, and many other parts of the world, men and women from ethnic minority groups are achieving great success. Their numbers are still relatively small, but they are growing.

Racial discrimination in institutions and in society as a whole leaves a wide "cultural divide" that members of minority groups have to cross if they want to achieve success. There is pressure to conform to certain expectations of speech, appearance, and behavior. African American tennis star Arthur Ashe complained of the stress he suffered from being "an ambassador" for the black community in the US. Everywhere he went, he felt it was his duty to act in a way that would prevent others from criticizing black people. He also admitted to toning down his regional accent, so it would be more "acceptable" to listeners.

The pressure to "fit in" can limit job opportunities. Skin color is one of the most obvious differences between people— even though it tells us nothing about a person's character or abilities. Even so, many institutions and companies are wary of hiring people from minority groups in case they do not "fit in." This is not logical, since the majority of non-white people in Europe and the US were born and educated in those countries, respectively.

Job applicants from ethnic minority groups can, of course, be better educated than applicants from the majority community. In 2013 in the United States, Asian students scored higher on average than white students on the ACT achievement test used in determining college admissions. But even where job applicants from minority groups are well educated, they can still find it difficult to gain job access due to unequal recruitment in many professions. For example, in the United States in 1987, people of color comprised only 12 percent of the total police force. While that number has risen to 27 percent in 2013, it is still below the 36.3 percent racial minority population in the United States.

Progress in the European Union

The EU has been called a "white man's club" in the past. Some member states classified people of non-white origin as "immigrants," even if they were born in these states. Until the year 2000, it had no laws protecting people from racial discrimination at work to match its laws on gender discrimination. The

Roma people, immigrants from northwest India who are often referred to as "Gypsies," have historically suffered violence and blatant discrimination in education and the workplace throughout the EU. Amnesty International reported in 2013 that there continues to be discrimination and violence against the Roma that was going unaddressed.

In 2000, the EU adopted the Race Equality Directive that prohibits discrimination based on race or ethnicity in employment, education, access to goods and services, housing, and health care. After the Race Equality Directive, concerted efforts by the EU have been made to improve equity among all races according to the following goals:

- Raise public awareness of anti-discrimination rights, with a focus on those most at risk, by involving employers and trade unions. Funding is provided to support such activities, along with a published a practical guide for victims of discrimination.
- Make reporting of discrimination for victims easier, by improving access to authorities.
- Ensure access to justice for those affected by discrimination with funds for training lawyers and non-profits representing victims of discrimination in how to apply equity law.
- Implement national strategies for Roma integration and protection with the general public.

Text-Dependent Questions

1. What is the difference between race and ethnicity?
2. Why was the European Union called the "white man's club," and what ways did it improve civil rights for people of color?
3. What is affirmative action, who does it help, and how does it promote equal opportunities?

 Research Project

Using the Internet or your school library, research the topic of affirmative action, and answer the following question: "Should affirmative action policies be used to help people of color get into colleges and secure jobs over 'more qualified' white people?"

Some think that since there is both direct and institutional racism against people of color, policies like affirmative action need to be employed to make things more equal in education and employment. Since white people have so many advantages in society, the gap in opportunities will always exist unless there is an intervention.

Others say people should get jobs or gain college admission only based on merit, what they have achieved. It is not fair to a white person who achieved more if a position is given to a person of color who achieved less.

Write a two-page report, using data you have found in your research to support your conclusion, and present it to your class.

4

Religion and Equal Opportunities

A person's identity is made up of many strands—including ethnic or national background, gender, age, and religious beliefs. It is hard to separate one strand completely from the others. Religion is often closely linked to politics and to issues of race or national origin. For this reason, it is rare to find discrimination against individuals or communities based simply on religion alone.

However, people with religious views that do not fit in with the majority views of their community may face discrimination. The Soviet Union, for example, was officially an atheist state. Jewish people who expressed a wish to emigrate from the Soviet Union to Israel—which had been founded in 1948 as a homeland for Jews—were treated as political *dissidents*. Their promotions at work were blocked, and some lost their jobs.

Pedestrians walk past a sign with an anti-Semitic message in the commercial district of a German town, 1935. The German-language message translates to, "Jews not wanted." Throughout history, people have been persecuted for their religious beliefs.

Soviet authorities argued that by expressing a wish to emigrate they were behaving like traitors.

In the United States, the Civil Rights Act of 1964 prohibited workplace discrimination based on religion, as well as on national origin, race, color, or sex. After the terrorist attacks on September 11, 2001, the US Equal Employment Opportunity Commission (EEOC) issued a reminder to employers which included the following: "The law's prohibitions include harassment or any other employment action based on any of the following:

- Harassing an individual because he or she is Arab or practices Islam (the religion that Muslims follow)
- Harassing a woman wearing a *hijab* (a traditional covering for the hair and neck worn by some Muslims)
- Refusing to promote an employee because he or she attends a mosque (Muslims' place of worship)."

 Words to Understand in This Chapter

caste—one of the hereditary social classes in Hinduism that restrict the occupations of their members and their associations with the members of other castes.

dissident—someone who disagrees with an established religious or political system, organization, or belief.

hijab—a traditional covering for the hair and neck that is worn by Muslim women.

Linking Religion and Politics

Belonging to a minority religious group can restrict work opportunities in other ways. In early twentieth century Northern Ireland, many of the largest companies were controlled by members of the Protestant faith, who were the majority in the country. Most Protestant companies refused to

In the years since the September 11, 2001, terrorist attacks, some American Muslims have reported being discriminated against in hiring and education.

Atheists march in a gay pride parade in Minnesota. In recent years, the number of people who do not believe in God or adhere to a particular religion has grown in the United States. According to the Pew Research Center, more than 3 percent of American adults considered themselves atheists in 2015. This was about twice as many atheists as a similar survey found in 2007.

employ Roman Catholics. This was not solely because of their religion, but because they assumed that they would have political sympathies with Irish Republicans—a group who wanted Northern Ireland to break away from Britain and become the Republic of Ireland, a separate, independent state.

Today, Northern Ireland is the only part of Britain where there are laws against religious discrimination. The Fair Employment Protection Act of 1976 requires all employers with more than 10 staff members to monitor the religious balance of their employees and regularly review their employment practices for any signs of discrimination.

When religion is linked to war and terrorism, this can also cause a backlash against workers of a particular faith. After attacks by Muslim terrorists on the US on September 11, 2001, many peaceful American Muslims faced hostility or harassment from work colleagues or classmates. Because they were Muslims, they were unfairly accused of being anti-American although they may have been upstanding citizens or even served honorably in the US military.

In the years since then, a number of projects to construct new mosques or Islamic centers have been blocked or delayed due to challenges from local communities. As of 2016, seven U.S. states—Alabama, Arizona, Kansas, Louisiana, North Carolina, South Dakota, and Tennessee—have passed laws that prevent the application or implementation of Islamic law (*Sharia*) in state courts. And in a Pew Research Center poll from 2015, 53 percent of Americans said they were very concerned about the rise of Islamic extremism in the United States. A consequence of this fear is that Americans have been less willing to accept Muslim immigrants and refugees from war-torn places like Syria, Libya, and Iraq. Many Americans are concerned that the US government is not able to properly screen the refugees to prevent terrorists from entering the country legally.

Religion and the Workplace

Religious faith can be the most powerful driving force in some people's lives. It is therefore very important that they feel able to carry out the prayers and practices that their religion requires.

Not all employers have been sympathetic to these feelings. This has led to cases being brought before the courts to enact changes in the law. In the United States and some parts of Europe, Muslim women have won the right to wear slacks instead of skirts with company uniforms, and Sikh men have won the right to wear beards unless they are working in a job where facial hair is prohibited due to hygiene laws.

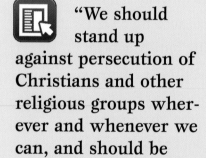

"We should stand up against persecution of Christians and other religious groups wherever and whenever we can, and should be unashamed in doing so."

—British Prime Minister David Cameron, 2015

Most faiths require that believers take part in public worship and attend services, rituals, and special celebrations. Where these do not coincide with the holiday times of the majority community, some employers have been unwilling to allow workers time off. In 1996, a British tribunal ruled against a company that refused to let workers take a half day off for the important

Christians demonstrate outside of a courthouse in Pensacola, Florida, in support of high school administrators on trial for allowing prayer in their school. Over the past decade some Christians have come to believe that there is a "war" being waged against their beliefs, as shown by the removal of the Ten Commandments from public buildings as well as battles over prayer in American public schools. Internationally, Christians are attacked for their beliefs in many countries, particularly in Africa and Asia.

Muslim festival of Eid. Employers who fail to make "reasonable" arrangements with their Muslim employees for daily prayers or allow Jewish people not to work on Saturdays also run the risk of discrimination claims.

Religion can limit job choice in a variety of ways. According to traditional Hindu beliefs, some jobs are "unclean" and can only be performed by people from low *castes*. People who do these jobs are not allowed to take on any others, for fear the things they touch might also become ritually "unclean."

One group of Scottish fishermen who belonged to a Christian sect refused to eat with non-believers—even on board crowded fishing boats. Perhaps not surprisingly, they found it hard to get jobs. But from their point of view, this was discrimination against their religious convictions.

Text-Dependent Questions

1. In twentieth century Northern Ireland, how did religion and politics mix when Protestants refused to employ Roman Catholics?
2. What guidelines did the EEOC establish to protect Muslims who were at risk for unfair workplace treatment after September 11, 2001?

 # Research Project

Using the Internet or your school library, research the topic of religious discrimination in the workplace, and answer the following question: "Should employers have to allow exceptions to workplace policies to accommodate workers' religious beliefs?"

Some contend that the employers should not have to make accommodations for religious beliefs because that would be giving special treatment to only certain workers or make a company less productive. They can choose to work at a place that will accommodate them.

Others argue that there are accommodations made in the workplace based on factors like pregnancy and special needs, so why not religion? In the US, a country founded on religious freedom, people should not have to stop practicing their religion because they are at work.

Write a two-page report, using data you have found in your research to support your conclusion, and present it to your class.

5

People with Disabilities

I n modern, industrialized countries, many people with physical disabilities do not receive equal opportunities to gain paid employment or full education. The situation is even worse in developing nations, where poverty and lack of modern technology make it harder for those with special needs to find work.

In traditional societies, physical, intellectual, or *developmental disabilities* are often seen as a cause of shame. People with disabilities may be hidden from view and not have regular contact with other members of the community. Some parents think there is no point in sending children with special needs to school or helping them learn to share in household tasks or any other kind of work.

These attitudes have been changing all around the world.

Even modern buildings are often designed without consideration for people with disabilities. But with a little thought, it should be possible to allow disabled people equal access to all public buildings, stores, offices, and other places of work.

In the developed countries, some equal opportunities campaigners are still advocating for *inclusion* policies where special education students are placed with general education peers. They argue that separate schools or classes from their general education peers allow attitudes of ignorance and prejudice to persist throughout the community. They also claim that separate schools may deny children the chance to reach their full academic potential.

Even when they have received an education and are qualified for a job, people with disabilities often have access to only work in low-paying occupations because of prejudicial beliefs, lack of accommodations, and limited transportation options.

In the twenty-first century, there is advanced technology with electronic devices, such as sophisticated communication aids, that allow more people with disabilities to make full use of their intellectual abilities and creative skills. Medical advances also mean that many people with special needs are able to expect a longer and healthier life than ever before. Yet

 Words to Understand in This Chapter

developmental disability—a diverse group of lifelong disabilities due to an impairment in physical, learning, language, or behavior areas that start before age 22 and include cerebral palsy, Down syndrome, and autism spectrum disorder.

inclusion (education)—an educational approach where special education students learn in the same schools and classes as general education peers.

person-first language—language that emphasizes the person, not the disability.

This worker has found a job in a woodworking shop, but many other people with disabilities are not so fortunate when it comes to the workplace.

many employers are still reluctant to recruit them and are sometimes quick to dismiss them when the need for accommodations arise.

Many people with disabilities would argue that they are not a "problem" for employers to cope with, but that the real "problem" lies in employers' negative attitudes toward them. They object to being called "disabled people" and prefer *person-first*

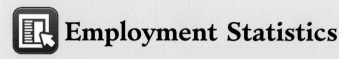

Employment Statistics

The US Census Bureau's 2011 American Community Survey revealed the following data regarding people disabilities and employment:

- Only 27 percent of people with disabilities were employed, compared to 65 percent of those without disabilities.
- Workers with special needs earn 64 cents for every dollar their non-disabled colleagues make.
- An average worker with special needs who has a high school or equivalent degree earns $6,505 per year less than their peers.

language like "people with disabilities" because they want to be defined by their humanity, not their disability. They argue that the real "disabilities" they face are the limitations placed on them by society, employers, and other individuals.

Battling Their Environment

People with disabilities say that having a job is an important sign that they are being treated as full members of the community. Trying to find work can therefore be a key part of a larger fight for equality.

However, in addition to facing negative attitudes, people with disabilities often have to struggle against an inaccessible physical environment. One student complained, for example, that the entrance to her university's library was through a heavy revolving door. There was a smaller door which her wheelchair could get through, but library staff had to leave their other duties to help her use it. This placed extra pressure on the staff, made her feel embarrassed, and caused delays for other library users.

Providing jobs for workers with disabilities would help to reduce the nearly 9 million people who receive annual disability benefits from the federal government through the Social Security Disability Insurance program.

With legal requirements for building accessibility in the US, many offices, stores, and factories are removing steep steps, narrow doorways, and cramped bathroom stalls that are unsuitable for wheelchair access. Ramps, elevators, and more space are making buildings accessible for everyone.

Laws Related to Disabilities

In many countries, civil rights laws now require employers to

 Wheelchairs versus Airplanes

Michael Oliver, in his 2009 book *Understanding Disability*, compared the situation of people who use wheelchairs to that of people who need airplanes to fly:

"We spend billions of dollars, yen, deutschmarks, and pounds every year providing non-flyers with the most sophisticated mobility aids imaginable. They are called [airplanes]. An [airplane] is a mobility aid for non-flyers in exactly the same way as a wheelchair is a mobility aid for non-walkers. . . .

We spend at least as much money to provide environments, usually called runways and airports, to ensure that these mobility aids can operate without hindrance. . . . Non-walkers are treated in exactly the opposite way. Environments are often designed to exclude us, transport systems that claim to be public continue to deny us access, and when we protest, we are told there is no money."

New technology helps people with hearing difficulties communicate in many different ways. But some employers are still reluctant to make full use of technology to allow disabled people to fulfill their potential.

make "reasonable adjustments" to buildings and work practices to offer people with disabilities equal access. These adjustments are often quite simple: rearranging workstations, installing extra lights, allowing flexible hours of work, or providing special parking spaces close to offices or factories.

Two landmark laws were passed by the US Congress that protected the civil rights of people with disabilities: In 1975, the Education for All Handicapped Children Act stated that

Transportation such as this lift-equipped van provides a way for people with disabilities to access their workplace, school, healthcare facilities, and community life.

children with disabilities were entitled to a free, appropriate public education and that each child's education must be planned and monitored with an individualized education program. In 1990, the Americans with Disabilities Act (ADA) prohibited discrimination against individuals with disabilities in all areas of public life including jobs, schools, transportation, communication, and all public and private places that were open to the general public. These two laws gave legal protection to adults and children with special needs, setting the standard for workplaces, schools, and public facilities.

Since then, companies have realized more and more that it can be good business to adapt their buildings and ways of working to employ staff with special needs—and attract customers with disabilities as well. By doing so, they find that they have a larger number of talented applicants to choose from while also expanding their customer base.

Transportation Problems

Transportation challenges make it difficult for many people with disabilities to find or keep jobs. Those who want a career may have limitations on where they can work and how often they can go. This is especially true if they live in big cities where driving cars can be slow and expensive; even people without disabilities find crowded buses and trains difficult to use.

Advocates for equal rights argue that with an inclusive approach and a fair share of public funds, transportation can be made accessible to all. Fortunately, with laws like the ADA, buses and trains are being fashioned with wheelchair accessi-

Pendik vs. Bursa match in the Turkish Amputee football league, April 2015

bility, and there are even training services for people with special needs to learn how to take public transportation. For those who are more severely impacted, there are also designated buses that provide door-to-door service.

Text-Dependent Questions

1. What was the point that Michael Oliver was trying to make with his airplane analogy?
2. Explain the specific protections provided for people with disabilities by the ADA and IDEA in 1990.

 Research Project

Using the Internet or your school library, research the topic of special education and inclusion, and answer the following question: "Should special education students be placed in all classes with general education students?"

Some believe that, should they choose to, special education students should have full access to the same classes, teachers, and social opportunities as their general education peers. It is the school district's responsibility to provide the supports necessary in general education environments for this to happen.

Others maintain that special education students may have more specialized instruction in separate, self-contained classes and with peers at similar achievement levels. They may thrive in smaller class settings or need extra attention that can be provided in those self-contained environments.

Write a two-page report, using data you have found in your research to support your conclusion, and present it to your class.

6

Other Types of Discrimination

Discrimination means unequal or different treatment or harassment that causes harm. In the United States and in most Western countries people generally have the right to equal treatment and opportunities, without discrimination or harassment. While discrimination based on race, gender, and disability may be the most common forms, anything that sets a person or group of people apart from others—including their age or their sexual orientation—may result in discrimination.

Age Discrimination

In many wealthy countries, most people retire when they reach age 60 or 65. They receive a pension from the government or their employer, or they live on money saved while they were at

Protesters and marchers rally outside Los Angeles's City Hall in November 2008, protesting the passage of California's Proposition 8 which banned gay marriage. The law was later overturned by the courts.

work. But should they have the right to keep working if they want to?

Many societies traditionally value older peoples' experience and work contribution. This perspective still exists in many poor countries where people often have no choice but to work for their entire lives merely to survive. In some Western industrial societies, however, the age of a worker has become a target of discrimination.

Discrimination against older workers becomes more serious during economic crises. Companies try to save money by reducing wage payments. Since older people are likely to occupy more senior positions that pay higher wages, companies often try to lay them off first.

Outside of difficult financial times, there are also general prejudices against older workers that exist. Some employers fear that they might be less familiar with modern technology. They might be less mobile physically and have health issues. They may be less willing to adapt to fast-changing work practices or learn new skills.

But there are signs that these attitudes are changing. Companies who have deliberately recruited older workers have

 Words to Understand in This Chapter

federal—of or relating to the central (national) government.

pension—an amount of money that a company or the government pays to a person who is retired or sick and no longer works.

Although most older people in the United States can look forward to receiving Social Security retirement benefits, some people will not make enough money to truly retire.

found that they can be particularly reliable and trustworthy. They may have emotional maturity and a wider experience of life, which can make them better at coping with problems.

Older women, who have already raised their families, are also less likely than younger female workers to need maternity leave. Employers who run stores say that many customers appreciate the "old-fashioned" courtesy of older staff.

What Laws Protect Seniors?

In the United States, the Age Discrimination in Employment Act of 1967 (ADEA) forbids age discrimination against people who are age 40 or older in hiring, promotion, firing, or pay. The law is specifically against discrimination against older workers: it is not illegal for an employer to favor an older worker over a younger one, even if both are age 40 or older. Though there is no federal law, some states also have laws that protect younger workers from age discrimination.

The Age Discrimination Act of 1975 prohibits discrimination on the basis of age in programs and activities receiving fed-

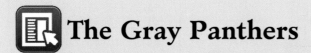 **The Gray Panthers**

In the US, a group of senior activists called the Gray Panthers demanded the same rights as younger people who had access to jobs and promotions. They objected to advertisements which included phrases such as "People over 50 need not apply" or "Bright, young person wanted."

The Gray Panthers were founded in 1975 by a woman named Maggie Kuhn, who had been forced to retire on her 65th birthday. The group took its name and many ideas from civil rights campaigns, especially the Black Power movement. The Gray Panthers believed in absolute equality for all people, regardless of age, color, disability, or sex and thought that doing useful work gave meaning and purpose to everyone's life. Being denied the chance to work took these away.

eral financial assistance, such as government offices and public educational institutions; it applies to all ages.

Although people in wealthy Western countries can look forward to a retirement pension, most countries are too poor to provide for older citizens this way.

Discrimination Based on Sexual Orientation

Over the past two decades, American society has seen an incredible change in attitudes toward people who are lesbian, gay, bisexual, or transgender (LGBT). Until relatively recently, those whose were attracted to members of the same sex, or had

Young people like these Canadian students are driving the movement for greater tolerance toward LGBT people. According to recent census data from the Canadian government, the number of same-sex married couples in Canada nearly tripled between 2006 and 2011.

Attitudes toward LGBT rights are changing in many Western countries, not just the United States. This photo shows an annual celebration held in Berlin, Germany, for the rights of LGBT people, and against discrimination and exclusion.

an unusual sexual orientation, could expect to be ostracized socially and, often, discriminated against professionally. Homosexual behavior was even a criminal offense, punishable by a jail term, in some states. People who "came out" to their families or friends often faced rejection and harassment. In 1987, according to the General Social Survey (GSS), an annual poll conducted by the University of Chicago, 75 percent of Americans felt same-sex relations are "always wrong."

However, attitudes changed during the 1990s and early 2000s. By the year 2000, the GSS found that the the number of Americans who felt same-sex relations are "always wrong" had dropped to 54 percent. By 2010, the number was down to 43.5 percent.

Today, more LGBT people are "out" than ever before. There are gay pride parades. There are magazines and newspapers devoted to LGBT issues. Openly gay Americans hold public office at the local, state, and national levels. Many popular television programs include gay characters who are depicted as normal people.

As American attitudes have changed, the federal government has made a number of policy decisions that protect the rights of LGBT people. In 2009, for example, President Obama signed an order that made the same-sex partners of federal employees eligible for benefits such as health insurance. The federal government also began to allow those who are in same-sex marriages or civil unions to file joint tax returns. In 2010, the president officially ended the "don't ask, don't tell" policy, which prevented openly gay or lesbian people from serving in the US military.

Important Court Cases

The US Supreme Court has also played an important role in protecting the rights of LGBT people. In 1996, the Court struck down a Colorado law that denied gays and lesbians protections against discrimination. Writing the Court's majority opinion for the case *Romer v. Evans*, Justice Anthony Kennedy said, "We find nothing special in the protections Amendment 2

Ukranian activists demonstrate for equality outside a government building in Kiev.

withholds. These protections . . . constitute ordinary civil life in a free society."

In the 2003 case *Lawrence v. Texas*, the Supreme Court ruled that a Texas law outlawing sodomy was unconstitutional because it violated peoples' right to privacy. This ruling invalidated sodomy laws in 13 other states, making same-sex sexual activity legal in every U.S. state and territory.

In June 2013, the Supreme Court ruled that the 1996 Defense of Marriage Act, a federal law that defined marriage as between a man and a woman, was unconstitutional. The Court found that the law violates the rights of gays and lesbians, and also interfered with the states' rights to define marriage.

In 2015, the Supreme Court ruled in *Obergefell v. Hodges* that same-sex couples have the fundamental right to marry and that states cannot say that marriage is reserved for heterosexual couples. "Under the Constitution, same-sex couples seek in marriage the same legal treatment as opposite-sex couples, and it would disparage their choices and diminish their personhood to deny them this right," Justice Kennedy wrote in the majority opinion.

Although there is far less stigma attached to being lesbian, gay, bisexual, or transgender than there was in the past, the United States still has a long way to go before it can be said that discrimination based on sexual orientation no longer exists.

 # Text-Dependent Questions

1. What did the Gray Panthers advocate for, and where did they draw some of their ideas from?
2. Name three advantages older workers might have over their younger counterparts.

 # Research Project

Using the Internet or your school library, research the topic of age discrimination, and answer the following question: "Should certain jobs be allowed to have an age limit?"

Some think that there should be no age limit on any job because all that matters is if the employee is able to do the work. Everyone should at least have the chance to prove themselves at a job.

Others say that for some jobs, like in construction or mail delivery, there should be an age limit because of the strength or mobility requirements involved. This would prevent older workers from being in unsafe situations, and companies would be more productive.

Write a two-page report, using data you have found in your research to support your conclusion, and present it to your class.

7

Can Equality Be Achieved?

We are all potentially guilty of discrimination against people who seem different from ourselves or have fewer advantages than we do. Civil rights activists urge us to think carefully about all we do and say. They tell us to make sure we treat everyone we meet with equal fairness, consideration, and courtesy.

Campaigners use the slogan, "If you are not part of the solution, you are part of the problem." Their argument is that individuals, businesses, institutions, and governments should all take action to make sure that everyone they deal with is treated fairly.

Other activists for equal opportunities encourage us to look beyond the people we meet face-to-face and consider how our attitudes and actions affect people in countries around the

Participants at a rally hold sign supporting the right of gays and lesbians to marry in Brisbane, Australia. As the understanding of the idea of human rights evolves, activists have supported protection of the rights of LGBT people around the world.

world. The economies of rich and poor countries are now linked through *globalization*. Thus, the personal choices we make—for example, in what we choose to buy—can affect equal opportunities at work for the men, women, and children in developing countries who make these products.

It is an unfortunate fact that, while awareness of equal opportunities has increased in wealthy countries, the gap between the rich and poor in the world has widened. The Pew Research Center reported in 2014 that 41 percent of global wealth is in the hands of 0.7 percent of the world's population, while 68.7 percent of the world possesses only 3 percent of the world's wealth. In the US, the poorest people are older women belonging to racial minority groups. They have suffered from unequal opportunities that result from a combination of gender, racial, and age discrimination.

Yet there are signs of hope. International campaigning groups have demanded the cancellation of debts owed by poor countries to rich ones. They hope this will leave poor countries free to improve education and health care—and to advance equal opportunities policies, if they so choose.

 Words to Understand in This Chapter

globalization—the development of an increasingly integrated worldwide community in business, technology, or philosophy.

solidarity—a feeling of unity between people who have the same interests, goals, etc.

The National Football League (NFL) established the Rooney Rule in 2003. It requires teams to interview racial minority candidates for head coaching and senior football operation jobs, though there is no quota or preference given to minorities in the hiring of candidates. People of color represented 10 percent of NFL head coaches before the Rooney Rule; since then they represent more than 20 percent of the head coaches. The rule is named for longtime Pittsburgh Steelers owner Dan Rooney; the Steelers hired their first African-American head coach, Mike Tomlin, before the 2007 season.

In wealthy, developed countries, tribunal cases like Neil Walkingshaw's, described at the beginning of this book, have shown how equal opportunities laws can help to make life better for many ordinary families, whatever work they do.

Is Education the Answer?

Most people would agree that education is one of the most important and effective ways of changing peoples' lives. It

Participants march in New York for gender equality and women's rights on International Women's Day, March 2015.

allows students to learn skills, gain knowledge, and win qualifications.

However, as we have seen in this book, getting a good education does not guarantee equal opportunities at work. Well-qualified candidates from disadvantaged groups still find it harder to get the jobs they want than applicants from majority groups. But there are signs that employers are beginning to recognize that well-educated people—whatever their background—are too valuable to turn away.

Education has proven to make a difference in getting a job

for racial minorities: In 2014, the US Bureau of Labor Statistics stated that only 7.5 percent of African Americans without a high school diploma were employed. That number jumps to 30.8 percent for those with a high school diploma and 33.2 percent for those with at least some college credit.

Thirty-nine percent of employed white people were in management or professional jobs, compared to 30 percent of African Americans, and 40 percent of Asians. Higher-level jobs that require a greater degree of education are no longer off limits to people of color.

Well-qualified women still face discrimination, even in educational careers. The World Bank reported that in 2012, 62 percent of high school teachers were female but only 30 percent of high school principals were female.

In developing countries, a good education can be even more important in escaping poverty and improving the chances at a good career. In those countries, the shortage of skilled professionals can sometimes lead to more equal opportunities for educated women than in wealthy industrialized nations. For example, there is a higher percentage of female university professors in Namibia, Bulgaria, and St. Lucia than there is in Australia, Spain, or the UK.

How Do People Protest?

Some campaigners stage protests to try to raise awareness about how their purchasing decisions affect local workers' lives. Some of these protests can be deeply controversial, such as the riots at international economic summits held from 1999 to 2001 in the US, Sweden, and Italy. Demonstrators protested

A women's rights demonstration in Iceland.

against wealthy governments' economic policies, the influence of the World Trade Organization, and the power of multinational corporations. Their aim was to show *solidarity*, or oneness, with poor and disadvantaged people groups worldwide. Unfortunately, the protests were marred by violence.

There are no easy answers to the problems of poverty and injustice, but by asking questions and putting forward their own points of view, peaceful campaigners and educators hope to make people aware of the importance of equal opportunities around the world.

 Text-Dependent Questions

1. What group of people in the US are the poorest and why?
2. Provide statistics that describe how education improves the employment outlook for people of color.

 Research Project

Using the Internet or your school library, research the topic of fair hiring practices, and answer the following question: "Should companies have to interview at least one person from an underrepresented minority group for job openings?"

Some take the stance that the inequality in hiring practices, including granting interviews, has to be challenged. By requiring interviews of minorities, people of color will at least be able to make their case for the job, and bosses will have exposure to quality candidates from minority groups.

Others maintain that bosses should not be forced to interview anyone since it is their company they are running. If they have to interview minority candidates that they were not thinking about in the first place, they may just go through the motions, with no real difference in the end.

Write a two-page report, using data you have found in your research to support your conclusion, and present it to your class.

Key Equal Opportunities Laws and Rulings in the United States

Racial, Gender, and Religious Discrimination

Brown v. Board of Education of Topeka, 1954
> Supreme Court declared separate schools for different races were inherently unequal and unconstitutional.

Civil Rights Act of 1964
> Banned discrimination on grounds of race, color, religion, sex or national origin in voting, public facilities, work, and education.

Civil Rights Act of 1968
> Prohibited discrimination due to race, religion, or national origin in the sale, rental, and financing of housing.

Civil Rights Act of 1991
> Provided for financial damages where people could prove job discrimination.

Gender Discrimination

Equal Pay Act, 1963
Stated that men and women doing equal jobs should
receive equal pay.

Title IX of the Education Amendments, 1972
Outlawed discrimination on the basis of sex in any fed-
erally funded education program, including sports.

Pregnancy Discrimination Act, 1978
Prohibited employment discrimination against female
workers who were (or intended to become) pregnant.

Discrimination against People with Disabilities

Rehabilitation Act, 1973
Banned discrimination in government jobs against
qualified people with disabilities.

Section 504 of the Rehabilitation Act of 1973
Students with disabilities were allowed accommodations and modifications to coursework that addressed
disabilities.

Education for All Handicapped Children Act of 1975
Students with a disability were entitled to a free, appropriate public education and individualized education
programs that addressed necessary areas of support

Americans with Disabilities Act, 1990
Banned discrimination in all jobs against qualified people with disabilities.

Age Discrimination

Age Discrimination in Employment Act, 1967
Protected people 40 years and older from job discrimination.

Age Discrimination Act, 1975
Outlawed discrimination on the basis of age in programs and activities receiving federal financial assistance.

Organizations to Contact

American Civil Rights Institute
P.O Box 188350
Sacramento, CA 95818
http://acri.org/

Amnesty International
5 Penn Plaza, 16th Floor
New York, NY 10001
http://www.amnestyusa.org/

**The Arc for People
with Intellectual and Developmental Disabilities**
1825 K Street, NW, Suite 1200
Washington, DC 20006
http://www.thearc.org/

Center for Equal Opportunity
7700 Leesburg Pike, Suite 231
Falls Church, VA 22043
http://www.ceousa.org

Center for Individual Rights

1233 20th Street NW, Suite 300

Washington, DC 20036

www.cir-usa.org

Equal Employment Opportunity Commission

Publications Distribution Center

P.O. Box 12549

Cincinnati, Ohio 45212-0549

www.eeoc.gov

**National Association for the Advancement
of Colored People (NAACP)**

4805 Mt. Hope Drive

Baltimore, MD 21215

www.naacp.org

National Organization for Women

1100 H Street NW, Suite 300

Washington, DC 20005

http://now.org/

US Commission on Civil Rights

1331 Pennsylvania Avenue, NW, Suite 1150

Washington, DC 20425

http://www.usccr.gov/

Series Glossary

apartheid—literally meaning "apartness," the political policies of the South African government from 1948 until the early 1990s designed to keep peoples segregated based on their color.

BCE and CE—alternatives to the traditional Western designation of calendar eras, which used the birth of Jesus as a dividing line. BCE stands for "Before the Common Era," and is equivalent to BC ("Before Christ"). Dates labeled CE, or "Common Era," are equivalent to *Anno Domini* (AD, or "the Year of Our Lord").

colony—a country or region ruled by another country.

democracy—a country in which the people can vote to choose those who govern them.

detention center—a place where people claiming asylum and refugee status are held while their case is investigated.

ethnic cleansing—an attempt to rid a country or region of a particular ethnic group. The term was first used to describe the attempt by Serb nationalists to rid Bosnia of Muslims.

house arrest—to be detained in your own home, rather than in prison, under the constant watch of police or other government forces, such as the army.

reformist—a person who wants to improve a country or an institution, such as the police force, by ridding it of abuses or faults.

republic—a country without a king or queen, such as the US.

United Nations—an international organization set up after the end of World War II to promote peace and co-operation throughout the world. Its predecessor was the League of Nations.

UN Security Council—the permanent committee of the United Nations that oversees its peacekeeping operations around the world.

World Bank—an international financial organization, connected to the United Nations. It is the largest source of financial aid to developing countries.

World War I—A war fought in Europe from 1914 to 1918, in which an alliance of nations that included Great Britain, France, Russia, Italy, and the United States defeated the alliance of Germany, Austria-Hungary, the Ottoman Empire, and Bulgaria.

World War II—A war fought in Europe, Africa, and Asia from 1939 to 1945, in which the Allied Powers (the United States, Great Britain, France, the Soviet Union, and China) worked together to defeat the Axis Powers (Germany, Italy, and Japan).

Further Reading

Branch, Taylor. *The King Years: Historic Moments in the Civil Rights Movement.* New York: Simon & Schuster, 2013.

Kendall, Gillian. *Nelson Mandela: A Life Inspired.* Boston: Wyatt North Publishing, 2014.

Kozol, Jonathan. *Savage Inequalities: Children in America's Schools.* New York: Broadway Paperbacks, 2012.

Nielsen, Kim E. *A Disability History of the United States.* Boston: Beacon Press, 2013.

Yousafzai, Malala. *I Am Malala: How One Girl Stood Up for Education and Changed the World.* London: Indigo, 2014.

Internet Resources

www.amnesty.org/en/what-we-do/discrimination/
Amnesty International addresses discrimination worldwide with news, information on issues, initiatives for justice, and statistics.

http://databank.worldbank.org/data/home.aspx
Statistics on issues such as education, health, and employment with demographics specific to gender, race, and age.

www.dol.gov/dol/topic/discrimination/index.htm
The US Department of Labor provides statistics and legal rights for people who face discrimination due to age, disability, race/ethnicity, and immigration.

www.infoplease.com/spot/civilrightstimeline1.html
US civil rights timeline with major historical events and laws from 1948 to present.

www.cdc.gov/lgbthealth/youth-resources.htm
The LGBT Helpline provides advice and resources for lesbian, gay, bisexual, and transgender people.

www.now.org
The US National Organization of Women offers links to women's organizations in many countries.

www.eeoc.gov/laws/types/
    The US Equal Employment Opportunities
    Commission's site lists discrimination types and laws
    protecting each group.

www.disability.gov/
    Practical and legal resources for people with disabili-
    ties on civil rights, community life, education, employ-
    ment, housing, technology, and transportation.

www.parentcenterhub.org/repository/specific-disabilities
    The Center for Parent Information and Resources has
    a list of specific disabilities, with definitions, tips, and
    resources for each.

*Publisher's Note: The websites listed on these pages were active at the time of publica-
tion. The publisher is not responsible for websites that have changed their address or
discontinued operation since the date of publication. The publisher reviews and
updates the websites each time the book is reprinted.*

Index

Numbers in ***bold italics*** refer to captions.

and cultural norms, 17–18,
   27–28
definition of, 11
movement, 14–17
and political change, 18–21
and protests, 93–94
See also discrimination
Equal Opportunities Commission
   (UK), 8, 49
Equal Pay Act, 16, 98
Equal Rights Amendment (ERA),
   15–16
ethnicity, 10, 41–42, 48–48, **50**
Export Processing Zone (EPZ), 26

Fair Employment Protection Act of
   1976, 61
Farenthold, Sissy, 38

"glass ceiling," 32–34, **35**, 36–37
   See also sex discrimination
Gray, Freddie, 51
Gray Panthers, 82

Harris, Eric, 51
Hinduism, 58, 64
   See also religious discrimination
Hussein, Saddam, 41

institutional racism, 49–51
Islam, 18, 58, **59**, 61–62, 64
   See also religious discrimination

Judaism, 57–58, 64
   See also religious discrimination

Kennedy, Anthony, 85–86
King, Martin Luther, Jr., 15
Kuhn, Maggie, 82

labor unions, 24, **25**, 26
Lawrence, Stephen, 50–51
Lawrence v. Texas, 86

laws, equal opportunity, 61, 85–86,
   97–99
   and age discrimination, 82–83,
      99
   and disability discrimination,
      12, 16–17, 72–73, 75, 98
   and racial discrimination, 12,
      13–14, 15, 54, 97
   and sex discrimination, 12,
      13–14, 15, 16, **29**, 97–98
   See also equal opportunities
LGBT rights, **79**, 83–86, **89**
   See also sexual orientation dis-
      crimination
Lilly Ledbetter Fair Pay Act, **29**

"maid trade," 30
   See also sex discrimination
Mandela, Nelson, 46–47
Meir, Golda, 37

Northern Ireland, 59, 61

Obama, Barack, **29**, 85
Obergefell v. Hodges, 86
Oliver, Michael, 72

person-first language, 68, 69–70
political change, 18–21

Race Equality Directive (EU), 54
racial discrimination, 10, 15, 53–54
   and apartheid, 42, 45–47
   and the "cultural divide," 52–53
   and ethnicity, 10, 41–42,
      48–49, **50**
   history of, 43–45
   and institutional racism, 49–51
   and job opportunities, 13–14,
      51–52, 53, **91**, 93
   and laws, 12, 13–14, 15, 54, 97
   and multiculturalism, 47–48
   and politics, 43

and wages, 28
religious discrimination, 10, 17–18,
    57–58, 61–62
    and job opportunities, 59, 61,
        62, 64
    and laws, 12, 15, 17, 61, 97
research projects, 21, 39, 55, 65, 77,
    87, 95
Rice, Tamir, 51
Roma people, 54
Romer v. Evans, 85–86
Russia, 20–21

segregation, **13**
    See also racial discrimination
sex discrimination, 7–9, 15–16,
    17–18
    and communism, 18–21
    and education, 31–32
    and the "glass ceiling," 32–34,
        35, 36–37
    and job opportunities, 13–14,
        17–21, 24–28, 29–31, 32–34,
        36–37, 93
    and laws, 12, 13–14, 15, 16, **29**,
        97–98
    and number of women work-
        ers, 25–27, 31, **35**, 36

and wages, 21, 23, 28
    and women in politics, 37–38
sexual orientation discrimination,
    10, **79**, 83–86
slavery, 44
South Africa, 42, 45–47
Soviet Union, 18–19, 20, 57–58

terrorism, 58, **59**, 61
Thatcher, Margaret, 37

Understanding Disability (Oliver),
    72
United Kingdom, 7–9, 43, 61
    and racial discrimination, 45,
        50–51, 52
United Nations, 14
United Nations Educational,
    Scientific, and Cultural
    Organization (UNESCO), 31

Walkingshaw, Neil, 7–9, 91
Wick, Ingeborg, 26
women workers. *See* sex discrimi-
    nation
Women Working in the Shadows
    (Wick), 26

About the Author

Frank McDowell studied history at St. John's University and worked with the non-governmental organization Human Rights Watch. This is his first book for young people.